Duet For

A Play

Tom Kempinski

Samuel French — London
New York — Sydney — Toronto — Hollywood

DUET FOR ONE

First produced at the Bush Theatre on 13th February 1980 with the following cast:

Stephanie Abrahams   Frances de la Tour
Dr Alfred Feldmann   David de Keyser

Directed by Roger Smith
Designed by Caroline Beaver

The play, presented by Ian B. Albery, Herbert Jay and Ray Cooney, opened at the Duke of York's Theatre, London, on 23rd September 1980 with the same cast, director and designer.

The action takes place in Dr Feldmann's consulting room

Time—the present

MUSIC

The Bach solo violin sonata, heard before the Curtain rises, is also played between each session, whether Dr Feldmann is playing it on his tape, as indicated or not.

ACT I

SESSION 1

Dr Feldmann's Consulting Room.

It is a calm, sober and cosy and welcoming room. Oak panelling on the walls; massive bookshelves full of psychiatric tomes, old and new; also rows of one or two psychiatric magazines. French windows lead to a large garden where roses and other flowers, etc., are visible. Between the bookshelves are pictures: some by patients, full of anxiety, others by talented modern representational artists. There are rows of tapes and records on shelves, which are played on an expensive-looking music-centre. There is a couch, with an armchair at its head. A desk, with a swivel armchair before it, is so placed that Feldmann never talks to his patients over the desk, but sits sideways on to it, talking to them with nothing between doctor and patient. A wooden filing-cabinet stands against the wall. The Doctor's family photos are on the desk and the cabinet. On a shelf and on the window-ledge are flowering plants. There are three small, expensive carpets, one by the door, one in the middle of the room, and one under the desk

Before the CURTAIN *rises, we hear Nathan Milstein playing a Bach solo violin sonata*

Dr Feldmann is sitting at his desk, writing notes. He can only be described as a typical German psychiatrist. He has been successfully analysed, and has that air of comforting wisdom common to his breed, which has nothing of the superior about it, but rather gives off the real feeling that one's problems are understood and sympathized with. He loves his work, the arts, life, and is still active in writing research papers and attending conferences. He speaks calmly and quietly, can smile, can sympathize in silence. He always looks at his patient when he or she is talking, except when he feels it might be too painful, say during a silence, when he looks down at his desk

After a few moments, his clock strikes three. He takes no notice and continues writing. He then closes the file he is writing in and consults his diary for the next appointment. He looks around the room, then goes to the armchair and pushes it into the corner. The doorbell rings. He gives the room a last look, then switches off the tape-deck, stopping the Bach music, goes out into the hall, and we hear him open the front door

Feldmann (*off*) Mrs Liebermann.
Stephanie (*off*) Dr Feldmann.
Feldmann (*off*) Please do come in. Just along the passage, the door on the left. May I help you through?

Stephanie (*off*) Thank you, that's fine.

After a moment, Stephanie appears in the open door in her electric wheel-chair. She is a tall, striking-looking woman, middle-class, well-educated. She had to rebel to realize her dream of becoming a musician, which has made her outspoken, often aggressive, witty, bitter and sarcastic some-times, and seemingly confident. She has courage, now stretched to its limit with the knowledge that she has multiple sclerosis and knows her worth as an artist. Underneath she is, of course, in despair. She and her husband are rich, so she wears good clothes, which are as bright, colourful and out-of-the-ordinary as she herself is. She moves some way into the room, stops, looks round at Feldmann, then moves on into the middle of the room

Where would you like me? This is the hot-seat, is it? Am I on the exact spot?

Feldmann (*smiling*) That is fine, if it is comfortable for you.

Stephanie Does a trapdoor open for the hopeless cases?

Feldmann sits down at his desk and smiles again. He takes up his pen

Feldmann You had no difficulty finding the door, I hope.

Stephanie Absolutely none. Your directions were perfect, thank you.

Feldmann Some people are confused by the door being at the side of the house up the little lane. But anyway . . . Now. May I just take down a few details; name, address and age, and so on?

Stephanie Didn't my doctor give you all that?

Feldmann You know; some persons make appointments and never arrive. I prefer to wait for them actually to appear.

Stephanie Afraid of the ghastly truth, are they? Hmmm . . . Well. My name is Stephanie Abrahams. I live with my husband at Fourteen, Bellevue Villas, N.W. eight, and I'm . . . Oh. You want our London address, presumably?

Feldmann Yes. That will be fine.

Stephanie Only we do have a house in Tuscany, where we live part of the year.

Feldmann The London address is quite all right. You can always give me the other address should we need it later.

Stephanie Fine. Well. I'm thirty-three years old, though David assures me I don't look a day over thirty-four.

Feldmann Thirty-three, yes.

Stephanie I have no children, fortunately, and I spend my day . . . Do you want all this now, right away?

Feldmann turns to face Stephanie

Feldmann Why do you regard it as fortunate that you have no children?

Stephanie Ah. The chance remark that reveals so much.

Feldmann continues to regard her questioningly

Well. I suppose it's fortunate because of all this. (*She indicates herself in the wheelchair*) This. Me.

Feldmann I am sorry. I do not quite understand. Do you mean that you feel it would distress your children to see you in a wheelchair?

Stephanie Yes. I suppose it would . . . Well, that's not exactly why I said that . . . Well I suppose it would distress them to see me like this, if they'd known me, you know, walking about properly, I suppose . . . Though some children might just take it naturally, I suppose . . . I'm sorry. I don't really know exactly why I said that. It just came out, I think. It's been one of the things I've just sort of naturally thought, I suppose. I really don't know exactly why I think it—thought it. Maybe it's not fortunate, really. Sorry. This is all a bit muddled. I don't know why properly, really.

Feldmann I understand. (*He makes a last note, then sits back just a little in his chair*) Now, Mrs Liebermann. . . .

Stephanie Miss Abrahams. I use my maiden name.

Feldmann Of course. I'm sorry. Please tell me why you have come to see me. (*He continues looking sympathetically at her*)

Stephanie Weeell—I came because my husband thought I was fairly upset with things and might benefit from some kind of I don't know, support or guidance, and I agreed with him.

Feldmann Do you always agree with what your husband says?

Stephanie No wonder people don't like people like you. That doesn't follow from what I just said. Why don't you ask me why we think I need support and guidance.

Feldmann Very well. And why do you. . . .

Stephanie No, no. It's all right. No. I don't always agree with what my husband says.

Feldmann In what matters do you not agree with him?

Stephanie Oh I don't know. Lots of things. He likes curry for one thing. Now ask me if I don't like Indians. . . .

Feldmann (*smiling*) I'm sorry. I have not made my question quite clear. Do you always agree with your husband on principle?

Stephanie Oh no. I never agree with anyone on principle. Just if I really agree.

Feldmann Do you agree with your husband on important matters in your marriage? Have you many things in common?

Stephanie Yes, we do.

Feldmann What things?

Stephanie Well. Music, of course, for one.

Feldmann And did you agree not to have children?

Stephanie Children? Oh children. Well. I don't know whether we agreed, exactly. It never came up. I suppose we were so busy with work, with working together, and so on, I suppose it just never came up. We never really discussed it, but I think we felt the same about it.

Feldmann And do you wish to have children now?

Stephanie Now? No. What, like this? No, I shouldn't think so. Why? Do you think I should? Is that what you're getting at? Is that what you think would help? I'm sorry. Is that what you're suggesting?

Feldmann I am suggesting nothing. I just want to hear what you feel.

Stephanie thinks

Feldmann makes notes on the desk next to him whenever he hears something he thinks is important; usually when Stephanie expresses a feeling. He does so with the least amount of disruption of his attention on her

So what is the problem you and your husband wanted you to see me about?

Stephanie Well. I do get a bit low, I suppose. I'm a pretty positive person generally. I don't usually sort of give in, if you know what I mean. And I've taken this thing pretty well, I think. But I do get low sometimes. Quite low sometimes, in fact. Not for too long, ever. But I do.

Feldmann What do you get—er—low about?

Stephanie About this. I've got multiple sclerosis. That's what I get low about. Wouldn't you?

Feldmann How long have you known that you had contracted the disease?

Stephanie A few months. Not long. About seven months, I think.

Feldmann And what in particular makes you feel low about the condition.

Stephanie What in particular? Well everything in particular; and everything in general too. What a question! You do know what multiple sclerosis is, I suppose?

Feldmann Oh yes. Of course. A disease which attacks the nerve linings leading to a progressive deterioration of the muscles . . .

Stephanie Right. Well there you are, then. It's bloody creeping paralysis, isn't it? No cure, no stopping it. No-one knows how fast or how long or any other damn thing about it.

Feldmann Yes. We know it attacks the nerve cells in the brain. It's true, I'm afraid, that we know very little more at the moment.

Stephanie There you are, then. So you know what I've got to look forward to, then, don't you?

Feldmann But you are not confined to your wheelchair, are you?

Stephanie Oh no. I can walk and everything. Look, I'll show you. (*She gets up and walks about, doing twirls and waving her arms*) See. Everything perfectly normal. But . . . (*She continues doing more of the same*) Well. It may not do it now . . . (*As she speaks, her left leg gives way under her and she falls*)

Feldmann Oh my goodness! Let me help you. (*He jumps up to help her*)

Stephanie There you are, you see. A very typical symptom, I'm told. Sometimes it's my fingers. Or my arms, anywhere.

Feldmann helps her back into her chair, and resumes his own

That's what makes me feel a bit low, see?

Feldmann Yes. (*After a moment*) Tell me, what picture do you have of yourself in the future which causes you particular pain?

Stephenie Oh I wouldn't go so far as calling it pain. It's just—well, you know, the usual; having to be pushed around by someone all the time. Put to bed; fed; rubber sheets. Just the helplessness, I suppose. The dependence.

Feldmann Hmm. On whom will you then be dependent so much?

Stephanie Not David, if that's what you're getting at. We can afford people. You know, nurses and things. We're rich.

Feldmann I see. (*Pause*) And tell me, please, what form does this feeling of being low take on exactly?

Stephanie Oh you know; just down. You must know, surely.

Feldmann Do you have feelings of anxiety?

Stephanie (*after a slight pause*) A bit, sometimes, I suppose.

Feldmann Do you weep?

Stephanie (*after a longer pause*) Yes, I do sometimes, as a matter of fact. It's rather funny, really. Sometimes I'm feeling quite all right and tears just suddenly start coming flooding down. And I don't really feel that bad in myself, actually. It's funny . . .

Feldmann And when you say that you feel "low". Do you mean that you get feelings of hopelessness, or gloominess? Can you describe it exactly?

Stephanie Oh it's never hopelessness. Not gloominess, really. Not as bad as that. Just—well low is the best word I can think of, I think.

Feldmann notes again. He then sits back a little again and says nothing, looking at the desk. She waits for his next question. When after quite a long pause it does not come she realizes he is not going to ask another, and looks down at her legs. The pause goes on. And on. And on. To break the embarrassment she asks a question

Is that the end of the interview?

Feldmann No. We have quite a lot more time left.

There is now another long pause, during which Stephanie experiences for the first time the painful feeling of being left to dangle by a psychiatrist as a means of forcing out one's own thoughts and feelings

Stephanie (*eventually*) To be honest, I wasn't all that sure about coming to see you, actually. As I said, David suggested it, but I said, "What can he do anyway?" Everyone with this illness must get pretty fed up at times. I mean, I'm not mentally ill or anything like that, so I didn't see what you could do really. But he said he thought you might be able to help ease things for me, so I agreed to come. But I wasn't sure really. (*Pause*) I'm still not, actually, to be honest. I mean without being rude, I don't see that there's much you can do, really. Do you, really?

Feldmann I don't know.

Pause—another long one

Stephanie Well. What I think really is this. I've got it and it's not going to go away for number one. Two; I'm bound to be a bit upset about it; every normal person would be, and I don't see why I should be any exception, and I'm not, frankly speaking. And three. The thing to do now is to look to the future. I can still live; I can still lead a life, even a very full life, come to that. I can teach. I know I wouldn't be able to demonstrate what I'm after with a pupil, but lots of teachers don't anyway: And I can always use tapes and records. I can be of more immediate help to my husband with his career. I can be secretary,

adviser, that sort of thing. Now that sounds a full life for a healthy
person, never mind a cripple. Anyway, that's the lines I've been thinking
along. So I honestly don't see there's much help I need, if I get all that
going. What do you think, Dr Feldmann?

Pause. Feldmann has not written anything

Feldmann Do you think of suicide at all, Miss Abrahams?

She is stopped in her tracks by this sudden change of topic

Stephanie (*quietly*) I can see I haven't impressed you much with my plans.
(*Pause*) Yes, I—er—I, um, did think of suicide, as a matter of fact. Yes,
I did. At the beginning, mostly, when I first heard; when they first told
me for definite at the clinic. It was a terrific shock, I suppose. I suppose
that's why. But David and I have talked it over so much, and he's so
sensitive and supportive, and then I began to find out properly about
the illness; you know, getting past the first panic and really finding out
how bad or not so bad it really is, and what with talking to David and
friends, I just came round to seeing a way forward. Just sort of a natural
resilience, I suppose. But I did think about it, yes . . .

Feldmann And do you still think about suicide?

Stephanie (*after a slight pause*) Sometimes—just a fleeting thought, now.
Just—just fleeting—sometimes—but just a flash in my mind, really. I
don't dwell on it at all.

Feldmann And when you first thought about it, and even now, perhaps,
are these serious thoughts of killing yourself?

Stephanie (*after a long pause*) I think they were, yes. I think so. I think I
might have meant it . . .

Feldmann But now you feel you don't? Now they are just flashes, as you
call them, because of your plans, is that so?

Stephanie (*after a slight pause*) Yes. I think so . . .

Feldmann does not come back

(*Quietly*) Do you think they're serious thoughts?

Feldmann does not reply. Pause

Feldmann Is there anything else you would like to say?

Stephanie (*after a slight pause*) I don't think so . . . No, I don't think so.
I can't think of anything. I think I've told you everything, more or
less . . . Yes. Yes. I have.

Feldmann thinks for a moment

Feldmann I think I would like to give you some medication to help you
with your depression. Have you ever taken any anti-depressant tablets
before?

Stephanie Do you really think I'm depressed?

*Feldmann makes a shrugging, non-committal gesture, as if to say "Call it
what you like"*

Feldmann Have you ever had such tablets prescribed before? You see, if you have, it could be a guide to what will be most effective for you.

Stephanie No. I never have, I'm afraid. They work differently for different people, do they?

Feldmann Exactly. It is a matter of trial and error. Some work better for some people than for others. Hmmm . . . (*He pauses to think for a moment, then begins to write out a prescription, and continues as he writes*) I would like you to take these two tablets. The first one, Nardil, you will take one in the morning and one midday. The second tablet, Imipramine, you take three at night, but you should begin by taking only one for two days, then two for two days and only then to the full dose. Is that clear? I will write all this down for you.

Stephanie No, that's quite clear, thank you.

He still writes the prescription and the instructions

Feldmann It is important that you leave five to six hours between taking the last of the Nardil and the Imipramine in the evening, because these tablets do not mix, and could cause serious side effects if you do not follow these recommendations. (*He finishes writing*) Also, the chemist will give you a card on which is written certain foods which cannot be eaten with the Nardil, and you should also avoid these too. Then I will see you again in two weeks, unless, of course there is any kind of problem in which case please don't hesitate to phone me whenever you wish.

Stephanie You really think I should come and see you again, do you?

Feldmann Well I would in any case have to discuss with you the way the medication is working. There might perhaps be changes necessary, you see. These things can only be discovered empirically.

Stephanie So it's just to sort of check on the tablets, is it?

Pause

Feldmann I think it is very important for you to discover your true feelings about your position at this moment.

Stephenie Do you mean some sort of analysis?

Feldmann No. I do not do psychoanalysis. But I really think that it is very important for you to understand these feelings you have. Very important. Indispensable, I should say.

Stephanie You sound worried. That's a bit worrying; for me, I mean.

Feldmann smiles wisely

Feldmann I did not mean to sound worried. I worry for all my patients.

Stephanie So I'm not too bad, then?

Again Feldmann raises his palms and shrugs his shoulders, as if to say: "Who can tell in this world?" He rises

Feldmann Let us see how the tablets work. I will see you in two weeks at the same time if that is convenient.

Stephanie Oh yes, that should be fine.

Feldmann Fine.

Stephanie drives her chair towards the door and Feldmann follows. She stops near the door

Stephanie I see you have a beautiful sound-deck and tapes and records. Are they music, or patients' confessions?

Feldmann (*with a little laugh*) Oh no. Music, of course. I am a great listener only, I'm afraid. And your instrument, the violin is my favourite instrument also. That is why your husband made your appointment with *me*, I believe. He had heard of my hobby when he made enquiries, I gather.

Stephanie Oh. (*Slight pause*) Well it's very nice that you like the violin too. It's such a—so . . . Well, good-bye, and thank you.

She holds out her hand. Feldmann motions her through the door, to show that he is taking her to the front door

Feldmann Please . . .

Stephanie and Feldmann exit, as the Lights fade to a Black-out

//   SESSION 2

The same

Stephanie's wheelchair is already on its spot, as is Feldmann. He takes her folder from beneath another one, opens it and looks at it for a moment. Then he leans back again a little, looks at Stephanie, but his pen is ready

Stephanie . . . a lot better than when I saw you last. Especially these last four or five days. Not that I was feeling that awful before, really, but, well, I don't know, I—er—I seem to be sort of in a better mood somehow. That's the pills working, is it?

Feldmann Can you tell me, please, in which way you are in a better mood exactly?

Stephanie Well, I don't know. I'm—I've—er—I've got sort of more energy, I think it is. You know; I'm brighter. Happier really, I suppose. More get-up-and-go, you know. Though as I said, I'm pretty much that way inclined anyway, of course.

Feldmann notes

Oh, there is one thing, though. Yes. I wanted to remember to tell you. I nearly forgot. I'm a bit irritable. I mean how can I say? I've got energy, but I'm a bit quick to be annoyed. You know, sort of if things don't go quite right, as I'd planned. For instance, I was phoning someone about something to do with David's work; nothing difficult, routine really and they sort of made out there was a problem where I honestly don't think there was one, I don't mean on purpose; just they couldn't quite see how to push it through and I got quite snappy with them. You know, really quite sharp. And a couple of times with David as well. Yes, I'm glad I remembered that. Is that me or the pills, do you think?

Feldmann Would you say this was a normal characteristic of yours?

Stephanie Oh no. Not at all. I mean, I can be a bit sarcastic sometimes, but this is different. This is—well it's real irritation, and that's new to me.

Feldmann thinks for a moment

Feldmann Hmm . . . Have you had this feeling continuously since the moment you left here, or more lately, in the last days?

Stephanie Well . . . (*She thinks for a moment*) From about three or four days after seeing you. But then it got more in the last few days. I mean, I got more energy then, but I got more ratty too, if you see what I mean.

Feldmann Yes, (*He notes*) I think this is the Nardil, which is not quite right for you. I will change this to another tablet called Parstelin, which is basically the same as Nardil, though a little stronger, but contains a mild tranquillizer. This is quite a common reaction with some people. This change will take away this irritation, I hope. And you must observe the same food restrictions as with the Nardil. You take it the same as the Nardil, morning and midday, one tablet. Yes.

Stephanie Oh yes, there was one thing. With the evening pill, for the first few days I got sweating and a dry mouth and sort of I could feel it in my blood type of a feeling. Is that all right? We were wondering why you hadn't warned me about that?

Feldmann Yes. These are minor side-effects which always accompany Imipramine in the first days, until the tablet takes full effect. You see, it is a cumulative effect with this type of tablet, which is why you felt the full effects only after eight or ten days. I don't like to mention these side-effects because some of my patients are very suggestible and will feel the symptoms I describe if I inform them what to expect, and then I do not get an accurate picture of what have been the real effects of the tablets, you see.

Stephanie Oh. I see.

He stops talking and leans back in his chair. She is a little more used to it after the last time, so after a lesser pause she begins to speak

Well. Anyway. Talking about getting to my real feelings about my situation, and so on, I was thinking about that since I met you, and really, I have to honestly, really tell you that I'm feeling really well about it. Especially now with the pills. I mean, I just don't know what else to say, because that's actually how I do feel. I mean, I've been really getting on with . . .

Stephanie's enthusiasm is not halted, but we can sense a certain over-excitement, covering what?

You see, what's been happening, and I suppose it's the pills that have made the difference, what's been happening, I've been actually getting on with what I had planned, which before I just only thought about without doing much about it, or hardly anything, actually. For instance,

I've already started taking pupils, and I'm still advertising for more. Of course, obviously, a person in my position doesn't take every applicant like an ordinary teacher, but I've taken two young soloists who already give concerts and who I knew were looking for further development, and, as I say, I really got down to it on the phone, and you know, properly with a notebook and pen and everything, and phoned the principals of the music colleges and some of our friends and drew up a list of people to audition, and I'll be doing that later this week and early next, and I'll take as many as I can handle with everything else I've got on now. Oh, by the way. When I said just now "a person in my position", I didn't mean to sound, you know, big-headed. I just wanted to point out that I only had two pupils so far because not because I'm not getting on with it, or holding back or depressed, or something, but because, you know, obviously it's only worth it for very advanced people to come to me, d'you see; it wasn't because as some kind of excuse for not doing what I said I'd do. Sorry; is that clear?.

Feldmann just looks at her

Right. Then with David, as regards helping him, I've taken to spending a few hours every day just following his secretary around, listening to whom she talks to, publishers, agents, the managers, the festival organizers, and so on, and just generally studying what she does and how she does it, so quite soon I'll be able to take over from her and be David's secretary myself, and what's so exciting about that is that it'll mean I'm making a real contribution to his career, and I've sent for a home-typing course, and I really think I'll finish up as the woman every great man is supposed to have behind him, I really do, and David's terribly happy about it, in fact he's thrilled with the progress I've been making all round, and he's very grateful to you, I may say, and rather pleased with himself that he picked you as well, the big-head, because it is the pills which have made the difference between just thinking about doing all this and actually doing it, don't you think?

Feldmann cuts her dead, after a slight pause

Feldmann This story is all not very helpful.

Stephanie is thunderstruck and then is furious. It shows in her face and grim-faced silence, and she bangs one knee rapidly against the other. Feldmann looks at her, then down at his desk, then back to her

Why are you so angry?
Stephanie I'm not!
Feldmann I feel that perhaps you are, though.

Stephanie stays grimly silent. Pause

I would like to hear how you came to play the violin.
Stephanie What!?
Feldmann How you started and your career and so on.
Stephanie That *will* be very helpful, will it? I must say, if you don't mind,

I don't see why you've just dismissed everything I've been doing and which we've been happy about, David and me, and with the help of *your* pills, what's more.

Feldmann does not reply

What did you want? Oh yes; how I started violin lessons. Well—well . . . (*She is slowly calming*) Now let's see. Let's try to tell this *very* helpfully.

She steals a look at Feldmann, who is still looking at his desk-top. She takes another breath

Weeeell—I don't really know where to start. I suppose it's . . . Well, my mother trained as a concert pianist, you see, in Paris, at the conservatoire. I never heard her play, of course, she died when I was nine, and—

Feldmann makes a note

—she'd stopped playing by the time she was eighteen anyway, because she married my father then, very young, and they weren't well-off, but apparently she was very good and set on a very big career, though she hardly ever talked about it and never seemed to miss it or regret it, because she was a very positive woman, very energetic, optimistic, but she never played again. But. She did used to listen to music, records and radio, which my father used to call "that noise", and she started me on the piano and violin at six, and was a wonderful support and very sensitive and warm about it, though she didn't teach me herself, she helped Daddy in the business, which was hand-made chocolates. You know how the big firms make chocolates in the factory with the chocolate poured over the centres on a conveyer-belt; well with hand-made chocolate, it's dipped in a small sort of baths of chocolate, which are heated by water, and you dip the centre, say nougat, or whatever, in, and put it on a tray and then, say, put an almond on top, or a pink sugar flower, or whatever. Well, Daddy had two small shops, and the chocolate was made at the back of the shops. Anyway I showed a lot of promise from the beginning and it was obvious I'd inherited my mother's talent for music, and she fostered it and nurtured it, which you have to do, and made sure I had good teachers and a general musical education alongside just playing the instruments, though I dropped the piano quite soon, at eight.

Feldmann And what did your father think about your playing?

Stephanie Oh I think he took it as a young girl's hobby like football or stamp-collecting, I think.

Feldmann He thought it was a bit of a noise too, perhaps.

Stephanie (*with a little laugh*) Bit, yes.

Feldmann But to you it was more than a hobby already?

Stephanie Oh yes. From the very beginning it meant everything to me.

Feldmann And does it mean everything to you now?

Stephanie (*surprised*) Well no. Of course not. It can't can it; I can't play, can I?

Feldmann (*quieter*) I just wondered if it still meant everything to you.

Stephanie (*with a little edge in her voice*) No. I said. It can't because I can't play. It can't mean everything if I can't do it, can it? Anyway . . . (*She brushes Feldmann's point aside with the pleasure of telling about her life as a violinist*) Shall I go on with what you asked me? I got up to a high standard very quickly, and I was the youngest person ever to win the Stern Scholarship for Young Musicians, of which I was and am *very* proud, and I was playing concerts as a soloist by the time I was thirteen, though of course I was still studying and still at school, as a matter of fact.

Feldmann You continued playing after your mother died quite normally?

Stephanie Oh yes. Oh I was on the road by then, nothing could stop me by then.

Feldmann But it must have been a great shock to you.

Stephanie Oh yes, of course, I was very upset and my father was nearly broken by it, but I carried on, oh yes.

Feldmann You went to an ordinary school, not a music school?

Stephanie Well, my father thought I should keep up my education, as he called it. Maybe he was right, I don't know, but anyway, it didn't stop me or do any harm. Some people it might have done, I suppose. Anyway, then I went and studied with Carrera in the holidays. .He's a wonderful teacher, though he's a great player tóo; though a lot of people don't know that, but he was wonderful, wonderful, fantastic, and then I won the Vienna International, youngest ever again, and that was it then, I was home and dry, and then I went to Oistrakh, oh he's such a character, you'd love him, he's so—so—such a character, you know, he talks like—he says things like, "we sing, do we not, mademoiselle? We sing of life, do we not; we sing.life itself, is that not what we are trying to do?" He spoke like music himself, like poetry it was, really; so lovely. I remember discussing the Mendelssohn with him once; it was lovely. . .

Feldmann How did you come to meet your husband?

Stephanie is annoyed at the interruption again

Stephanie Look. I thought you wanted to know how I came to play the violin. You did ask me that, didn't you? I'm not going deaf as well as stiff, am I? You did actually ask me that just a moment ago, right, am I right?

Feldmann Certainly, yès.

Stephanie Well you're a rotten audience, did you know that? I thought you shrinks just sat there and let us nuts get on with it. I was rather fairly well known, you know. I mean the story can't be *that* boring, is it?

Feldmann smiles

Feldmann I was also interested how you met your husband.

Stephanie Well all *right*! But can't we . . . Oh what the hell. I suppose you think you know what you're doing. It is a bit private this, you know. Is it really important? Relevant?

Feldmann just looks at her. He smiles

Well . . . *(She pauses as her happiest memory floods into her thinking. Quietly)* It was lovely, actually. I was at the B.B.C. television studios, waiting to give a concert that evening, and I was just doing a bit of rehearsing in an empty studio I'd found, and I played the Bach G minor sonata, and at the end David was standing at one of the studio doors, and he just walked over and asked me to play some Beethoven with him. Have you seen David? You know he's very tall, very thick blond hair swept back—*(she laughs)*—very "young music genius", but he's so broad as well, you know, not skinny like Tortellier, he's very powerful, like a boxer or someone and he was there to do an *Omnibus* programme, and he'd just heard me. Of course I recognized him, though I'd never met him, and we played the Beethoven, and it was just like nature, and I played like a . . . like Paganini and Heifetz all rolled into one, really, and at the end there was this long silence as we looked at each other. And then suddenly a lot of people were clapping and cheering; they were lighting men and actors—I don't know—and they'd crept in and listened behind pieces of scenery and lamps, and they were stamping their feet and cheering, and David and I just sat where we'd stopped playing and looked at one another, and that night we went to bed, first time for me, *not* for David, I might add—*(laughing)*—and that was like Beethoven too. You do know Beethoven, don't you. Lots of heavy chords and plenty of climaxes! *(She laughs out loud with happiness)* And three weeks later we were married. The papers called it a fairy story, but it wasn't . . . *(She stops, wide-eyed, remembering)*

Feldmann I'm sorry? You say it was not a fairy story?

Stephanie smiles

Stephanie Fairy stories don't happen, do they?

Pause

Feldmann I was going to ask you before what your father felt about your career as a concert artist.

Stephanie takes a moment to snap out of her reverie

Stephanie Hmm? Oh. Well he was pretty impressed when he saw what kind of money I was earning.

There is quite a long pause, as Stephanie buries herself in her happy memory, and Feldmann waits for some development. In vain

Feldmann I was wondering if you are at all concerned that your illness could affect your relationship with your husband?

Stephanie hardly hears, but what she hears, she does not like

Stephanie Sorry, I didn't quite catch that?

Feldmann I was wondering if you might be concerned that your illness could affect your relationship with your husband?

Stephanie (*puzzled, slightly annoyed*) No. (*She looks straight at Feldmann*) No; not at all. (*Pause*) Why should it? Why should I be? (*Pause*) Well, of course, it'll mean some changes, that's obvious. Any fool can see that. Well. They'll just have to be made. In fact, as I've already *told* you, they *are* already being made. What—how should it affect our relationship. What do you mean, "affect our relationship?"

Feldmann What are these changes that you feel will occur?

Stephanie (*after a slight pause; taking a breath*) Look. I don't want to seem rude, or something, but isn't that just a bit of a stupid question? I mean the first change is clear and obvious even to the simple-minded, which is that I can't play David's music, and I'm already making the necessary changes required by that new situation between us, which is that I'm training myself to be David's secretary, as I explained all of one second ago, and which even a moron wouldn't need to ask of half of a husband and wife team who used to make music together. The second change, which is equally clear, limpidly clear, even to the mentally retarded, I should have thought, is that our sexual habits will change, depending on the progress of the illness, and what stage it's reached. Would you like me to go into details? Next change I feel will occur are things like being pushed in a wheelchair, which, if you were to look in this direction, you would see has already occurred, while David will walk, and will have to hold my hand with his arm slightly straighter, because I'm a bit lower down; is things like lowering the surfaces in the kitchen, which has already been done, and other, minor matters. You see, strange as it may seem, David and I have actually discussed these problems together as if we were actually real, live, grown-ups, though there may be people around who think we're just silly children, and we've worked out ways of coping with these changes because you see, we happen to love each other. Does that go any way to answering your question, Dr Feldmann, at all, does it?

Feldmann is completely unmoved by her sarcasm. He pauses for a moment, considering what strength his next question should have. Then quietly

Feldmann You see; what I had in mind actually was something like this: it was music that brought you together with your husband, and which, perhaps, at the deepest level, has kept you together. Or, at least, you may, perhaps feel that this is the case. And if this was true, or you believed it to be the truth, then you might, perhaps, fear that, because this link has been broken, at least in the form in which it originally existed, that this fact could jeopardize your marriage in some way, you see? Also, your husband loves music and is a musical person himself, while your father was not, nor did he like your musicality to a great degree, as far as I understand what you have so far told me about him, and this difference between these two men in your life must have been, I imagine, a great satisfaction for you; perhaps a very deep satisfaction and of great significance. And therefore it is for these reasons only that I wondered what your feelings were now that you are no longer a practising musical person for this man who chose you, you may feel, precisely for your great gifts, which echoed his own and complemented them. I am concerned, therefore, that we uncover any fears or anxieties you could be feeling, that your husband might now feel less close, less committed, shall we say, or you could even have worries about his leaving you, because you were no longer the same person he met, and so on. These would be normal reactions to the situation you now find yourself in, you see. And I wanted us to consider the possibility of such quite normal feelings, if you were experiencing anything along these lines, perhaps.

There is a long, long, long pause. Stephanie is incredibly angry, because Feldmann has hit the nail, but she cannot admit it. So she experiences all this as an insult, particularly after what she has just said. So she winds herself up to explain to him calmly again: but she is so full, she can only be calm for the first few words; then she explodes

Stephanie Dr . . . (*She clears her throat*) Dr. . . . (*She clears throat*) What —er—what. I'm not clear . . . (*Suddenly she explodes*) JESUS CHRIST! What is this! What the hell is going on here, what are you bloody after anyway? I come here in good faith, I come because there may be a problem, I come willingly, openly . . . Do you have many patients at all, Dr Feldmann, eh? Do you? Have you? I mean, *do* you, because as far as I can see, you must be sending people out of here to see other doctors as fast as their legs, or their wheelchairs can carry them. I think you must send them to other doctors with a whole *new* set of illnesses and problems which you have specially and skilfully created by sheer determined hard work and bloody bloody-mindedness and insensitivity and rudeness, which I wouldn't have thought, though I am, of course not the great white-coated expert on the sub-conscious that you obviously mistakenly think you are, I would have thought . . . I mean I *wouldn't* have thought that those were the best attributes for helping people who are suffering, and don't think you've cleverly made me confess that I'm suffering, because *I'm not, repeat I'm not: not, savvy!* I mean is this some deeply clever, significant way of trying to break up my marriage, is that your recipe for my condition, is that it, have I caught on? Or have you some potty theory you're testing out on me that by upsetting me . . . What . . . I have tried to tell you, I have *told* you . . . I mean, I . . . (*She stops abruptly with her mouth open, because her mind has gone blank. She is stuck there for a moment, but the anger brings her line of thinking back to mind*) Yes. Look! David, that's my husband David, you know, David Liebermann, you know, the world-famous composer, that Liebermann, right? He has a wonderful career, right? In fact a brilliant, gleaming career, in fact, because, if I may say this in the presence of another one, he is a genius. He is undoubtedly one of the greatest composers of his age.

Feldmann (*quietly*) Is this now a source of envy for you?

Stephanie *Will you shut up! Will you just bloody well shut up for a minute, will you?* Will you, or not, because if not, I'm leaving. Now which is it to be, hmm? (*Pause*) Right. Good. Better. Now. (*She is quieter, with the* *assurance of his silence*) Will you try, please, and grasp this, just this little fact; things are good between us. In fact things are good for me. I am ill, but I am making the best of my condition. I have made plans to cope with the changes that my condition brings with it. These plans are sensible, they have been worked out *with* my husband, they are working, it's O.K., it's fine, *molto bene, molto allegro con vivace*, etc. etc., right? It seems to me that all you're doing is look on the black side, which isn't there, except in your head somewhere, or is about some mythical, possible person, who definitely isn't me. *I* am getting on just fine, see? We are making progress, we are working things out, we are getting down to it. I mean, come to think of it, it's you that gave me the pills, for God's sake, well they're working, they're having an effect, I mean they're not placebos, are they, I'm not imagining these improvements, am I, so they're actually working as you presumably want them to, and you just go and run everything down, that's what you're doing, running things down, while you've given me pills to make me cheer up; it just doesn't make sense. It's crazy. Now can we just make a little gentleman's agreement, could we, between us, and it's that I'm coping. Believe me; take my word for it, honest, cross my heart and hope to die, all right. I am. Really. No, seriously, Dr Feldmann. I am. I'm coping. I'm making a go of it. I have to and I am. Couldn't we please just take that as read?

Feldmann Like your mother had to also, to cope; to make a go of it, the best of a bad job.

This hits her like a revelation. Slight pause

Stephanie (*quietly*) I never thought of that. . . .

Feldmann Like you, she was forced by circumstances to break off an apparently brilliant musical career. Perhaps you feel your father stopped her. But she, like you, was a positive, cheerful, forward-looking person, so she too got on with it and made the best of her life.

He smiles. He has not said it to be one up on her, but to help her accept other suggested paths for inner exploration. But Stephanie does not even notice his little dig

Stephanie It's amazingly similar, isn't it. I'm—I'm really quite, very . . . (*Pause*) Funny. I never once saw the similarity. Yes. I do think of her as being forced to break off her career by circumstances, and I do blame my father sometimes, but then in a way I can't because she loved him, and they were poor then, which wasn't either of their faults, and she had to choose, and she chose to be with him, and that meant helping in the first shop. And I did get my positive side from her, it's true. And now I'm forced into the same situation as her. Funny . . . (*Pause*) You're not suggesting that I got this illness to be like her, are you?

Feldmann Oh no, certainly not. This part of the similarity is just a terribly unfortunate coincidence.

Slight pause

Stephanie So what are you suggesting?

Feldmann It would be natural for you to follow her example anyway, as in many respects all girls do. But I think that perhaps with her early death, and at a time when you were coming to young womanhood, this might be even more to be expected.

Stephanie Yes? So?

Feldmann Then perhaps we could learn something from other parallels in your lives, and also from areas where there are not, as yet, any parallels, do you think?

Stephanie But—but—I don't see what. I can't see what.

Feldmann Well. We could consider these two facts. First that you have had your careers interrupted, and secondly that you both have adopted this very positive attitude towards this fact. Is it not possible, though, that both of you harboured, unconsciously perhaps, other feelings underneath this so determined healthy approach towards your respective situations.

Stephanie Well. If she did, I never . . . She never gave any sign of it. And as I've explained, I've really adapted well, as far as I can see. So I can't see anything there. What else do you think? What else?

Feldmann gives her a long, slow look, as she once again determinedly overlooks her inner feelings; and rushes past what he is trying to get her to face, in order to find a solution to her tensions in some safer area

Feldmann (*after a pause*) All right. Let us consider for a moment your rôles as mothers; the question of children.

Stephanie I haven't got children. I don't see a parallel there. How do you mean?

Feldmann Your mother decided to fulfil her rôle as mother, but used that rôle quite naturally to give an outlet for her musical side through you. Perhaps you are considering such a thing also?

Stephanie No. No, I haven't. I mean I really hadn't considered it. Does that mean . . .? Sorry I don't see . . .

Feldmann But you would agree that such a thing, to release your musicality through children of your own, you would agree I suppose that such a thing would be possible?

Stephanie Well, I suppose so.

Feldmann Even a natural reaction, perhaps.

Stephanie Well. Perhaps.

Feldmann pauses a moment before delivering another bomb with his quiet insight

Feldmann (*more quietly*) Then perhaps you would consider, and I ask you only to consider this as a possibility, hypothetically, for the moment. Perhaps you would consider that, if such a reaction might be a natural one, that you do have this reaction, that you have considered the possibility of children to help in your dilemma, but that something else, other fears perhaps, are blocking this path for you.

Stephanie (*just a fraction tetchy*) It's a possible hypothesis, I suppose. So?

Slight pause

Feldmann (*quietly*) I know that some of the ideas I put to you are very painful, Miss Abrahams. But I ask you to take them into your heart if you possibly can, all the same.

Stephanie just looks at him. Slight pause

(*Quietly*) Would it be possible for you to consider that you have thought of children as a way of fulfilment, but that you may be having doubts about your ability as a cripple, as you said, to be a real mother. Would it be possible for you to consider also, that such doubts are all the more painful, since you are, perhaps, thinking that these children would also bind you closer to your husband, whom you *do* fear you may lose, and that such children could be the cement to stop you splitting apart, because you *do* fear . . .

Stephanie rises to her feet, trembling, interrupting this intolerable man's filth

Stephanie *Nothing is splitting apart! Things are under control! Everything is under control. Everything is perfectly under control.*

She rushes towards the door, but her leg gives again and she falls. Feldmann is up to help her. From where she lies she shrieks

DON'T TOUCH ME! DON'T YOU TOUCH ME! DON'T YOU COME NEAR ME! (*She gets up and walks back to her chair, falls again, gets up, gets into the chair, and drives it to the door, where she turns to him*) *I CAN MANAGE!!*

Stephanie exits

Feldmann stands for a moment. The Lights fade to a Black-out

SESSION 3

The same

Stephanie and Feldmann are both in their seats, he comfortably leaning back slightly, she tense, and sitting with her back to him

Stephanie . . . in fact, if David *hadn't* asked me to come back again, I do assure you, you wouldn't have seen me for dust again, ever. However, he *did* ask me to come back again, so to please him, I have, and he asked me to apologize, so to please him and only to please him, I'll do that too. I'm sorry.

Feldmann smiles

Feldmann I don't get the feeling from your tone that you mean that.

Stephanie In which case my tone is an accurate reflection of my thinking, Dr Feldmann.

Feldmann I understand. So you came back purely because your husband has asked you to do so?

Stephanie You've understood my English perfectly. For the first time, I might add.

Feldmann But you did come for your own reasons too, of course.

Stephanie Ah. Sorry. You obviously *didn't* understand my English perfectly. *Mea culpa* entirely, I'm sure. Very well, then, I'll try again. (*She now articulates each word very precisely with gaps between syllables*) I—own-ly—ca*me*—be-cauze—my—huz-band—ask*t*—me—toooo. Iz—th-a*t*—cle-ar—nowww?

Feldmann Excuse me. I understood you to say that you never agreed with your husband on principle. If you agreed to what he asked on this occasion, presumably you therefore had your own reason for doing so, independent of merely his request.

Stephanie Oh brilliant. Quite superb, in fact. Speaking as an ex-violinist, I must say, I always found logical people to be so tremendously, incredibly, *boring*, *if* you don't mind me saying so.

Silence. Pause

I'm not sleeping well. I suppose it's those bloody other tablets you changed me on to. I either want to come off them entirely . . . No, come to think of it, I don't. I want some sleeping tablets.

Feldmann The irritability has disappeared, I take it.

Stephanie Yes. As a matter of fact, it has. Though not with regard to your good self, I might add. There it has increased considerably.

Feldmann Are you waking up in the night, or do you have difficulty in getting to sleep at all? Or both?

Stephanie is still completely frozen towards him

Stephanie I have difficulty getting to sleep. Once asleep, I sleep perfectly well.

Feldmann I don't think sleeping tablets will be necessary. What time . . . ?

Stephanie Still terrified I'll kill myself, are we? Very bad for the great doctor's image, I imagine. But since I imagine most of your patients have committed suicide, perhaps one more will hardly register in the statistics. As long as they keep coming, and the money keeps flowing in, hmm? How can I kill myself anyway, on the pills? I thought they were precisely designed to lift your mood, so that you *didn't* kill yourself.

Feldmann It's true. They do lift your mood. If you were still, however, distressed in your thoughts, you might stop taking them, and then . . .

Stephanie And then it's cutting-wrist time, is it?

Feldmann Is that how you imagine doing this to yourself?

Stephanie imitates Feldmann's gesture of shrugging his shoulders and turning her hands face-up, back at him

What time in the evening do you take the Imipramine?

Stephanie Despite the fact that, of course you're quite right, and I'm a *desperate* case and can't cope at *all* at the moment, despite this *tragic* fact, I'm actually so busy all day and in the evening too, that I always

forget to take them six hours after the others, and I take them when I
go to the bathroom before going to bed, actually.

Feldmann Ah yes. I thought so. It is the Imipramine that is stopping you
getting to sleep. Taken late, it affects some persons in this way. I think
if you were to take them earlier by the amount of hours you find it
takes you to get to sleep, you would find you had no further trouble.

Stephanie (*sarcastically*) Wonderful!

Silence

Feldmann Is there anything else you would like to discuss?

Stephanie No.

Feldmann You do not wish to say anything about the matters we touched
last time?

Stephanie No.

Pause

Feldmann Would you prefer to end this session early and leave now?

Stephanie Frightfully big of you. I have paid my money, and shall stay.

Feldmann But you do not wish to talk about anything at all.

Stephanie No.

Feldmann I see. (*Pause*) I wanted us to discuss your father, as a matter of
fact.

Stephanie Really.

Feldmann Yes. I feel that you have mentioned him a number of times, but
have not really said fully what you felt about him, what really went on
between you, and so on, and yet you must have much to say about him,
as he brought you up and so on. This is an important area we have to
look at more closely.

Silence

Did you love your father?

Stephanie Of course.

Feldmann Did you get on well with him?

Stephanie Very.

Feldmann But I received the impression that he was not very interested
in your musical side.

Stephanie You're quite mistaken.

Feldmann Oh really. Are you saying he approved of you becoming a
concert violinist?

Stephanie Exactly.

Feldmann has written no notes. He knows this is all pointless

Feldmann Miss Abrahams. We are really wasting our time with this type
of defensive behaviour, you know.

Stephanie Good.

Pause

Feldmann I recall another patient I once tried to treat who also would not speak. The poor man wasted an enormous amount of money for nothing. He made me feel extremely guilty, I remember.

Stephanie I suppose you're going to tell me that because he didn't talk to you, he went off and lead a miserable life, are you? Is that the moral for me of this little fairy tale?

Feldmann smiles

Feldmann Quite the contrary, as a matter of fact. He married an extremely rich woman, and all his symptoms disappeared. It was a very chastening experience for a young doctor, I assure you.

Stephanie Don't think you're going to soften me up with these boring little tales of a failed doctor's life story. I'm fully aware of your little game, believe me.

Feldmann Sometimes the silence is as painful for me as it is for my patient, I assure you, Miss Abrahams.

Stephanie How simply *awful* for you, Doctor.

Feldmann (*sighing*) It's true, I assure you.

Stephanie Oh give it a rest, will you! You're lying. You're just telling lies to try and win me round. What do you take for me? You're lying; it's as plain as plain chocolate, mate . . .

Stephanie stops in mid-sentence, and stares into herself. Feldmann waits a moment for something else. When nothing comes, he probes

Feldmann (*quietly*) What is it, Miss Abrahams?

Stephanie (*quietly, half to herself*) That's what I used to say to my father, when he invented some nonsense to try and get back into favour with me. That's what I used to say . . .

Slight pause. Stephanie's sarcastic defence is breached

Feldmann Do you feel your father was often false with you?

Stephanie (*quietly*) Yes. Pretty often. Yes. About my playing mostly, yes.

Feldmann In which way, precisely?

Stephanie He'd upset me saying something unpleasant about my playing, and then, when I cried, he'd pretend he hadn't meant it. I wasn't convinced.

Feldmann When your mother was alive, she supported you in your endeavours of course, you said.

Stephanie Totally, yes.

Feldmann Then how did you manage when she died?

Stephanie I coped, I was upset. We've been through this before.

Feldmann Excuse me, what I meant was, how did you manage with regard to your playing?

Stephanie Well—I suppose, at first, I suppose it was all right, because Daddy just went on regarding it as my little girl's hobby. (*Slight pause*) Then—well, then I started to say I wanted to take it up seriously, for life, sort of thing. Well at first he just sort of pooh-poohed it, you know, "Yes, yes, tut, tut," and so on. And I started to dig my heels in and then the rows started. "I'll stop paying for your lessons; a wandering minstrel's no life for my daughter; scraping cat-gut for a living", and so on. So then I said I wouldn't do any school-work if he stopped me. (*During this speech, we more and more see a new side of her: it is the side that underpins her sarcasm and determination; a great strength, which grew out of her determined struggle against her father to pursue what she* had *to pursue—her music. She fought and triumphed. As the speech progresses, she reflects more and more this iron in her soul*) I remember that row; it was one tea-time, after school. I had shepherd's pie. He was so furious when I said I wouldn't do my school-work. He couldn't believe I'd stand up to him, I mean cross him like that. He hit me. Here. And then he said that settled it, he *was* going to stop paying for my lessons—and he did. Actually did stop paying for my music lessons. And I didn't write an essay, do a sum, paint a picture, read a book; nothing. That went on for five weeks and three-and-a-half days. Then he paid again. (*Pause*) Then he tried snidey things. He said he was tired after working all day for me; didn't I have any consideration practising when he was trying to get a bit of rest? I went and practised at a friend's, so he stopped that too. I think he wanted me back in the house to have me on hand to continue the battle. Then he tried saying my playing was absolutely wonderful, and I didn't need to practise so much; I was up to standard already. Incredible isn't it, really; so blatant, so transparent. I didn't budge an inch; three hours a day, every day, rain or shine. *And* did my home-work too. Round three, he developed mysterious illnesses. Always very vague, but very painful; migraines, heart-murmurs, back-pains, so I had to do everything around the house; cramps, I don't know. One day I told him to hurry up and die, 'cos it would save a lot of doctors' bills, and I could use the money for my lessons. I remember that was during a cramp period. The cramps vanished miraculously and he knocked me over the blue armchair . . . (*She stops again, hard-faced. Then she softens a little*) He was just a little businessman, really, you know. He couldn't really grasp it. He couldn't really grasp what I was about at all; it wasn't . . . He just didn't, I don't know; there just wasn't anywhere in his head that could grasp it, you see. But he was determined. And he was bitter. And he was lonely too, I suppose. And guilty. Everything jumbled. But very determined. "I want my child to be something better than me; better than a small-time shopkeeper; is a scraper something better, is it? Is that something better? It's for people's spare-time. Something to discuss over dinner for the top people. But it's not serious. Be a doctor, a surgeon, they have women on boards of directors now. Be *something* useful. This for fun, for amusement." Oh it was unending. (*She toughens*) And I fought him every inch of the way. Every word, every comment, every innuendo, every insult. I read up about women artists, asked my teachers for examples. I went out every day and brought back some weapon to fight him with. (*Pause. Not regretfully*) And gradually he weakened. He'd sulk. Long silences. Days he wouldn't speak. But I spoke. When he had nothing to say except sit there feeling sorry for himself, I'd come in with some story of a famous musician playing to some king or some famous person, or winning a prize. I piled on the attack the more he retreated, because he'd suddenly find new energy and come out with some violent, bitter bit of rubbish he'd heard somewhere from some idiot in the shop; a pianist committing suicide; that woman who played in the nude; artists were no better than scum, they were the most promiscuous group of people on the planet, it said so in the *Daily Mirror*, or some rag, *Tit-Bits* I think one bit of rubbish he found in. And then Round four was crying and begging and pleading and what would become of him in his old age. I told him once he could come to my concerts on a stretcher. He was so respectable. So narrow. So petty in his horizons. Ugh! I hated him for it . . .

Long pause

Feldmann (*quietly*) And yet, wouldn't you have liked to please him, if it had been possible, if you could have, perhaps.

Stephanie (*her voice hard*) I know you're the expert on the subconscious goings-on here, Dr Feldmann, and maybe I did want to please him, but if I did, I didn't let myself know it. I didn't let it get into my thoughts. I knew what I had to do. It was meant, see. Meant. It was meant. And no hand-made chocolate maker was going to stop me playing, see. Not my father, not the Pope, not the Chief Rabbi, not even God, if he'd joined in the objections. I knew where *I* was going. (*Slight pause*) You won't be surprised to hear that I can't eat chocolate. Not since a long time ago.

Long pause

Feldmann So you won?

Stephanie Yes! I won. Bach or Plain Assorted. Which do you think's for people's spare-time. Oh yes. Definitely. I definitely won.

Feldmann You showed great determination in the face of severe pressure, wouldn't you say so?

Stephanie Yes.

Slight pause

Feldmann (*quietly*) As you are showing it now, perhaps. You believe it can overcome all opposition, perhaps. From inside, from outside. Is that so?

Stephanie Let's just say that it helps, wouldn't you say?

Slight pause

Feldmann Tell me, please. What would you say you had gained as a prize from your victory?

Stephanie smiles a radiant smile from deep inside

Stephanie Oh Dr Feldmann. Look around you. Look at your tapes and

your records. You know them; you listen to them. You don't really
need.me to answer that, do you?

Feldmann Nevertheless, I should like to hear what you have to say.

Stephanie But why? Why? We know. We both know. Millions of people
know, and we know. I can't tell you better than you know yourself.

Feldmann (*after a slight pause*) Miss Abrahams. You have just told me
of a great struggle you engaged in to achieve a certain goal. I would
like to hear your feelings about the results of that struggle.

Stephanie Well. I don't feel sorry for Dad, or guilty, if that's what you
mean.

Feldmann No, no. I meant music, Miss Abrahams.

Pause. Stephanie fills like a balloon with joy

Stephanie (*slowly at first*) Well—music. (*Pause*) Music. Music, Dr Feldmann, is the purest expression of humanity that there is. Because, you
see, it's magic; but real magic, true mystery, not trickery. You can say
it is sound, as speech is sound, as bird-song is sound, but it isn't. It's
itself. A piece of music which expresses pain or sorrow, or loneliness, it
sounds nothing like what a lonely man says or does, but it expresses it,
and even better than the person does. Magic. You see, there's no God,
you know, Dr Feldmann, but I know where they got the idea; they got
it from music. It is a kind of heaven. It's unearthly. It lifts you out of
life to another place. That was my prize, that's what I won.

*Stephanie is utterly radiant. Feldmann has built to this moment. Now he
picks the fruit of his skilful husbandry*

Feldmann (*quietly*) And now?

*Stephanie carries her radiance over into her next speech. But quite soon
tears begin to flow, and she cries, but not from the depth of her high-flown
feelings, but from their opposite, as, from deep, deep down, her feelings
answer Feldmann's question because she is admitting for the first time that
she can no longer make music, and the pain of that. So as she persists, by
determination, in her sublime feelings on the surface, the depth of her
anguish shows through, forces its way to the top, try as she may to keep it
down. She talks through her sobs, over them, coughs them down, wipes them
away, cries and talks at the same time; but gradually the truth asserts itself,
and destroys her great pretence*

Stephanie Now I shall pour my magic into others; who will make my
sounds for me. They'll come to me because they know I climbed the
peaks, made peaks of my own that weren't even there before, and then
climbed those too. (*She begins to cry*) At first they will only be able to
scale the lower slopes. And then, in struggle and great joy, in pain and
ecstasy, they'll climb too. And they'll do it because I shall pour my
magic through their souls; my hand will be near to steady them when
they threaten to fall or turn aside and my strength will give them
strength. (*She is suppressing and releasing gulps of anguish by now*) I
have a special room in my house where I practise. It's blue . . . (*Shuddering*

gulps of weeping shake her entire body) I—can never—never—play —the—the—the—violin again! Never—never—never—never—never again. What do hulks do, Dr Feldmann? (*She is in despair*) You see, Dr Feldmann, you can't change this condition with determination.

The Lights fade to a Black-out, as—

the CURTAIN *falls*

ACT II

SESSION 4

The same

Stephanie and Feldmann are already in their usual places. Feldmann is looking at his desk, she looks very pointedly around the room, though it is clear she is not really interested. She is demonstrating "I'm very bored with this whole business". As opposed to the various smart outfits she wore in Act I, she now looks bedraggled, both as regards her clothes, and her face and hair; as though she is no longer bothering
Suddenly, aggressively and violently, she drives her wheelchair round the room, rucking the carpet, and making the wheels pass very close to Feldmann's feet. She finishes where she began. A long silence

Stephanie "Hey diddle diddle,
        The cat and the fiddle,
        The cow jumped over the moon.
        The silly doctor laughed to see such sport,
        'Cos he's simply an ignorant loon."

A long silence

And I'm *not* going to apologize for missing the last two appointments, if that's what you're waiting for, so tough shit, mate. *And* David didn't ask me to, *and* if he had, I still wouldn't anyway. Clear?

Silence

And while we're on the subject, would you mind *not* phoning me up in my own, private home and pursuing me like some crazed hound after the smell of a fox, or something. I know you need your money, and all that, but would you be kind enough to let *me* decide if I want your services in future, and not phone up at all hours of the day and night when I'm in the middle of doing things, thank you.

Feldmann I phoned twice simply to see if you might be in need of a talk It's my normal practice when a patient misses an appointment. I apologize if it caused you annoyance or embarrassment.

Stephanie Embarrassment!? What do you mean, "embarrassment"? It didn't cause me any embarrassment. I just don't happen to like every Tom, Dick or Harry thinking they can break into the privacy of my life at the drop of a volume of Freud, or whoever your little god is, that's all. So you can cut that right out, Mister. See?

A short silence

Feldmann Did I interrupt a lesson you were giving?

Stephanie Mind your own fucking business, would you, please. (*Silence*) You know what your trouble is, Dr Feldmann? I mean we've spent a lot of time and money looking at what's supposed to be wrong with me. Fair's fair; let's take a little look at one or two of your little short-comings, shall we? Your trouble, Mister, is that you're what Stern would call "a pain in the tuchus", which means the arse, for your information. To be specific about your major symptoms and leaving the minor ones aside for the moment, first, you suffer from telephone-mania; second, you have this maddening habit of looking at your boots, instead of having the good manners of looking at the person you're sitting opposite and third, you keep sucking those fucking Meggezones when you haven't even got a cold, and fourth, and by no means least, this phoney German accent you put on, to give people the idea that you're some wizard mid-European guru, or something, is, as far as I can see, a definite sign of schizophrenia, or at best, delusions of grandeur. Now if you'd care to come to *my* house once or twice a week and pay *me* fifteen pounds a session, I'd be glad to try and help you with these maddening habits, and make you as normal as the rest of us. What do you say, hmmm?

Feldmann It is certainly true that many of my patients go through times when they find me extremely irritating. That is certainly the case, Miss Abrahams.

Stephanie You're damn right it's the case; and you're the case, mate, believe me. (*Silence*) Well. Since you are clearly re*fus*ing to speak, which is *always* a sign of blocked thoughts or feelings, as you know, I shall have to help you out by saying something. You'll be delighted to hear that I'm hardly taking the pills any more; or very irregularly, anyway. So there; how does that grab you, Dr Frankenstein. Will your monster now turn into a vampire, or something? A little worried, are we?

She waits with triumph in her eyes for Feldmann to be upset, but he has been there so often . . .

Feldmann And how are you managing without them, may I enquire?

Stephanie Extremely well. Frightfully well, as a matter of fact. Better than ever. I think they were half the cause of the trouble, actually. In fact I'm thinking of going to someone who knows rather better what drugs to administer for my condition. I don't think . . . I think this case is just a *wee* bit beyond your competence, actually; don't you, if you're honest with yourself for once?

Feldmann It's a matter of opinion at this stage, I think. We can only judge by the final results of the course of treatment.

Stephanie Oh I *see*. So *that's* what this is, is it; a course of treatment. Ah. Well now. Now we know where we are, don't we? And how is the treatment going, in your deeply considered opinion? Satisfactory, is it? Successful, would you say?

Feldmann I would really like to recommend that you resume with the tablets on a regular basis.

Stephanie Ah yes. The profound moral question of suicide; I knew there was something else I'd been meaning to make your day with. I've been seriously considering it again, and I wanted your professional opinion as to the best and least painful and most foolproof method. I couldn't *bear* to do it and then wake up with you looking over me with that sickly sympathetic expression on your face. Though it might kill me from shock, I suppose, so maybe it would turn out all right anyway. What are your feelings on the subject, though? (*She moves towards Feldmann, and puts on a German accent*) I really vould like to know vat you sink and feel about ziss kwestion, Doctor Feltmann, hmm? Vat do you sink, hmm?

Feldmann answers so straight, it is like an arrow

Feldmann I think suicide is a waste of life, and I have dedicated my whole life to the preservation and improvement of life. So I am utterly opposed to it. Completely and utterly opposed and against it.

Stephanie cannot keep up her bitter antagonism and sarcasm in the face of such a principled and deeply felt answer, and bows her head. She moves away.

Pause

How have your plans been progressing? I mean the lessons and helping your husband, and so on?

Stephanie is subdued

Stephanie They haven't.

Feldmann waits. Stephanie repeats her point sharply

I *said* they haven't been progressing.
Feldmann Have you changed your plans then?

She does not answer the question directly, but talks half to herself

Stephanie Bloody untalented bastards coming into my house scratching their violins, sounding like a fucking bitch in heat, the pair of them. I told them to piss off and get some talent from somewhere, before they came round me with their fucking noise.

Pause

Feldmann Perhaps you could find some more gifted pupils, hmm?
Stephanie What do I want to teach some idiots the violin for! I'm not a fucking teacher! Let them go and find some failed bum; they can teach them if they need the money. I'm a performer, not a bloody teacher. Or I was, anyway. But that still doesn't make me a failure, a failed nobody. Let 'em find a teacher. I don't want their scraping in my house, I can tell you. Bloody people!
Feldmann And your idea of helping your husband with his . . .
Stephanie He's got a secretary!
Feldmann I only thought you . . .

Stephanie I said he's got a secretary! Tart! Bows and scrapes round him as if the sun shone out of his arse.

Pause

Feldmann Have you had any other ideas for the future?

Stephanie Why don't you all leave me alone, will you! Just why don't you all get off my back, pushing me to this and that and the other. Just let me be and let me do what I want, will you? David's the same; "but what *would* you like to do then, darling?" I'd like you both to just *leave me alone, savvy!*? Just piss off and leave me in peace, the pair of you.

Pause

Feldmann I remember I read a book by a doctor at one time. He was a follower of Adler, I recall, though his name escapes me for the moment. The book was very interesting and written by a very humane mind. In it he describes the phenomenon of the ambitious businessman who arrives at the age of forty and suddenly finds that he has realized all his ambitions, and there frequently followed a profound crisis or what the lay person might call a nervous breakdown. And he explains how he treated these people by turning their thoughts and aims away from themselves to the service of others, and how immediately they found their sense of life being meaningful restored. I remember an example he quoted of such a man who now rose early from his sleep and before going to work would visit one of the major railway terminals and offer to carry the heavy baggage of one of the passengers as they came off the train. I was very moved by this. "How to be happy though human", the book was entitled. It is a real contribution, I think.

Stephanie Oh I absolutely see what you mean, Doctor. Absolutely.

Feldmann Ah, good. I am glad.

Stephanie Oh yes. Plain as a pikestaff. You want me to get up early every morning and go to Victoria and carry someone's suitcase. Right on, Doc.; just the thing for multiple sclerosis, right? Really terrific, I should say.

Feldmann My purpose in mentioning this little example was this: it is frequent in neurotic persons that their illness, crisis, or whatever it is that is blocking their development, creates such pain, often greater than the worst physical pain one can imagine, that it makes them focus continuously inward on themselves, while the solution they seek is often to be found in concerning themselves in the needs of others. And then, miraculously, they find the deepest gratification, which they believed for so long they could only find by being preoccupied with their own inner trauma. This is the moral of my little tale, as you would say. I am not suggesting that you take up a new career with Pickfords removal people.

Feldmann gives a little laugh. Stephanie looks at him

Stephanie Well I think that's all balls!

Feldmann Miss Abrahams, you must try to grasp that the feelings of irritation and frustration you feel, come as a result of the enormous development you made when you were here last. To allow yourself to bring such feelings into your conscious mind, must inevitably cause a great turmoil and confusion within you. But these are actually a sign of movement, of change, and therefore herald further development. Please try, if you will, to see this positive side to your present feelings.

Stephanie Balls, mate! You know so much, don't you? You know it all, don't you? I mean, I was no mean violinist, but I didn't think I was God, you know. But you do. Big development last time? Huh! You mean blubbing about not being able to play any more? I knew that all along. What's so great about that. And now I'm going to suddenly out of this confusion and turmoil, as you call it, I'm going to discover a whole new self and a whole new life, am I. Well what is it then, if you know so much, eh? What the fuck is it?

Feldmann I do not know. It is hidden. We must uncover it. Together if you will allow it.

Stephanie Mystical bullshit, Feldmann. Mumbo-jumbo, Mister.

Pause

Feldmann What does your husband feel about the present position?

Stephanie How the hell should I know! He's composing his atonal gibberish eight hours a day, driving me mad. Very considerate, considering how I'm feeling and being ill too.

Feldmann just looks at her

And what are you staring at, may I ask? I suppose you think his music's the greatest thing since the sliced loaf, do you? Half your shelves are full of it, are they? Oh, I get it. This is another one of your big break-throughs, isn't it? I'm revealing to myself for the first time that I'm jealous of my husband's music, aren't I? Well, you must be out of your mind if you think I'm jealous of that—(*she hums a send-up of modern music*)—fucking rubbish. Well, he could compose his rubbish somewhere else couldn't he, he doesn't *have* to rub it in by going on doing it right under my nose. Or he could sound-proof his room, or something. Anything. But oh no. Twelve-tone, mathematical shit all day long; breakfast, lunch and tea. Not a *thought* as to what I might be feeling. Oh no —rotten bastard!

Slight pause. The clock strikes four

Feldmann I am afraid we have no more time this week. Our time is up.

Stephanie What! What did you say?

Feldmann Our time is up.

Stephanie And I have a few more painful truths to get off my chest, if you don't mind.

Feldmann waits. She says nothing at all. Feldmann rises

Feldmann We will continue at your next session, shall we?

Stephanie looks at him long and hard. She wheels her chair round so violently she has to correct its path. As she makes for the door, the outside bell rings. She turns her head

Stephanie Another fifteen pounds at the door for you, master.

Stephanie sweeps out

Feldmann puts her file away, takes another one, and puts it on his desk. He then goes to the door, as the Lights fade to a Black-out

SESSION 5

The same

Stephanie and Feldmann are in their places. She looks even more scruffy than in the previous session. For the first time, we see her in a real depression. Feldmann knows it

A short pause

Feldmann We are very quiet today I see.

Stephanie does not react even a flicker from her position of staring at the ground in front of her. Pause

Is there anything in particular that is troubling you at this moment? (*Pause*) Have you reconsidered recommencing any of the plans you had made when you first came to see me?

Pause. Stephanie speaks from far away

Stephanie Saying "*we* are very quiet today"; that's how they talk to children, isn't it.

Feldmann Perhaps you are making an impression on me like that of a child.

Long pause

Stephanie I gave my violin away yesterday. (*Pause*) I don't think I was much of an artist really. I don't think I was much good really. (*Pause*) I used to be absolutely still; just used to tremble to the music ever so slightly. I think people used to think that was romantic. I think it fooled them. I was a fraud, really. (*Pause*) String quartets I should have played really. I think that was my mark really. (*Silence*) They just liked the image really. David did too. They all just fell for the image. (*Pause*) When I first got the illness, I used to think "well at least I did it; I got there, I made it. They can't take that away from me". (*Pause*) But I didn't make it. It was the image, of course. (*Silence*) I'm wearing the same underpants I had on the last time I came. (*She has the same dress as well*) I haven't washed them since. They smell a bit now. It's a nice smell.

Silence. Silence. Silence

Feldmann What has made you feel that you weren't much good as a violinist, Miss Abrahams?

Pause

Stephanie David and I haven't made love for quite a time. (*Pause*) Mostly I just sit, you see. Or I stay in bed and David comes up and is very nice to me.

Feldmann rises, goes to the tape-deck and puts on a tape of the cadenza from the Beethoven violin concerto. As the orchestra starts to come in at the end of it, he switches off. Pause

I was flat.

Feldmann Miss Abrahams, do you know the purpose of life?

Stephanie laughs a little contemptuous laugh. Her rage has brought her slightly out of her depression

Stephanie Do you know the one about the man who spends his whole life looking for the meaning of life, going from one wise man to another, but none of them know it, until someone tells him that there's a guru in a cave up Everest, he's about eighty by now, and sure enough, in the cave there's a little, naked man sitting cross-legged. So he asks him the meaning of life, and the little man doesn't answer for about ten hours, and then he whispers, "The meaning of life is chicken soup." Well the old man's furious and says, "You mean to tell me I've spent the whole of my life looking for the meaning of life, and now I come to you up Everest, and you're telling me it's chicken soup?" And the little guru doesn't say anything for ages, and finally he looks at the other man and says, "You mean it's not chicken soup?"

Feldmann laughs. They look at each other for a long moment

Feldmann Miss Abrahams. In the early days of man's history on this planet, he had to struggle greatly against enormous adversity, as you yourself are struggling now. But this man's struggle was mainly a physical one against the elements; storm, cold, floods which destroyed the harvest, the sun which would not shine to ripen it, and so on. And so he would ask himself, why have I been set down on this piece of dirt to endure such pain and suffering for myself and my tribe and my loved ones. And in his misery, he sought a purpose to his hardship outside of himself, since he saw none in life itself. And so he told himself that this purpose, for purpose there had surely to be, since all his difficulties could surely not be meaningless—he told himself that this purpose was an idea in the mind of God. God had created him and set him to work for his own ends, and many and various were the explanations of what exactly these purposes of God's were, and sometimes, when he could not even think why God should give him such a hard life, he simply said that the purpose was a mystery, insoluble in this life, but to be revealed in the next, the better, happier life. And this troubled man persisted in his belief for thousands of years of hard and grinding living. I am not concerned here to debate the truth of this heavenly Father, and if a patient finds his way with the help of these ideas, I am content.

But now this man can see the possibility of his struggle for life becoming less and less hard. He begins to conquer the elements, his life is longer, he sees the chance of his family growing up healthy and happy. And now the true purpose of life reveals itself, not needing the unfathomable mystery of the Lord, but plain, before our eyes. Because the purpose of life, Miss Abrahams, is life itself; yes, the very struggle to live itself. Man labours, as we have seen. What is this labour, but his activity to transform his world, to overcome the problems it places before him, so that he may have a longer and a better life? He no longer waits for the river to dry up in the summer so that he may cross it; he builds an iron bridge and crosses in all weathers. He does not cross the Atlantic in a tiny sailing boat, fearing each day to fall off the edge of the world; he flies to New York in three hours and when he arrives, he sits in an air-conditioned house, and discusses with others the computer chip, which can further alleviate his labours. In other words, the purpose of life now shows itself to be the life-activity itself; man's own achievements are his purpose and his reward. He transforms the world into a more agreeable place to inhabit, and in so doing, he grows in knowledge, and hopefully one day, in wisdom. We need no outside purpose, for we have it in our very living itself. Watch a child develop; it grasps at the world greedily, like a madman released from a jail. It touches and grabs at everything; it breaks and bangs and throws everything in its love of everything it sees and feels and hears and tastes and smells. It seems to lust, to thirst for life. Do you need to ask it what the purpose of all this joyous activity is? If it could understand you, it would laugh at you and say, "The purpose is doing it, because I want to knock down the brick house which Mummy made; and later I will want to build it up. I love this; I see others doing it, I feel myself doing it and it is wonderful. I am changing the Universe. What stupid questions you ask." Now to you, Miss Abrahams. As primitive man was the subject of the blind forces of nature, so you too are at the mercy of the dark forces of your unconscious mind, at the moment, they have you in their power; you sit around, you complain, you say you can do nothing. But as that primitive man set about transforming his hostile forces to his own purposes, so you too must now engage yourself in a life activity, to master your dark forces. To succeed will be a great labour; but succeed you can and must. You say you had your only purpose, and now it is gone forever, and indeed it is a deep loss for you and for us also. But there are a thousand, a million endless other purposes you can enjoy: the sun on your body, reading, writing—even with a pencil held in your mouth to operate a typewriter if necessary. It is so difficult, I know, Stephanie, but it is so easy too. The tree of life has more than merely one wretched apple on it, believe me. Reach! Pick. No supermarket has such a choice of wares, believe me. I have seen so many, and they are not even the harvest of a single branch.

Stephanie seems not to have been listening

Stephanie (*after a pause*) I'm having an affair, you know.

Feldmann is genuinely surprised. It is the last thing he would have imagined as a reply. He pauses fractionally

Feldmann Oh yes?
Stephanie (*flatly*) Yes. He's a totter.
Feldmann I'm sorry?
Stephanie A totter. The man who comes round in a lorry and collects scrap-metal. Don't you have them round here?

No reply

We fuck on Thursday afternoons, which is on his regular round, and then any other time that his business commitments allow. Which is quite often, usually, actually. You see, it depends if he's picked up, say, a load of lead or something valuable, or whether it's just the usual run of old fridges and stoves, and so on. Copper's very good, of course. That's worth usually two or three fucks, and brass is worth a couple too, mostly. If I'm *very* bored I go out and buy some copper piping, and then he's up me for the whole afternoon.

Feldmann is looking straight into her eyes

Well copper's . . . Fetches a good price, you see. I'm learning a lot about metals, actually. He's a very big man, very strong. Apparently he was on the buildings before he went into business on his own account, as he says. I don't think he ever washes, because he's incredibly smelly all over, but he feels very good to touch, and I just turn my head away, because he doesn't go in for kissing hardly at all, so it's not a major problem. (*Slight pause*) I never have a climax, but I pretend. He fucks me like a sack because I'm a little restricted. I think that's what turns him on. He likes music too. In fact, he says he's very musical and that everyone says so. Standards he likes. Jack Jones is a genius, he believes, and he's asked me to come and hear him sing at his local on a Saturday evening, but I haven't been free to yet. I'll have to wait till David has an appointment at that time.

Pause. When Feldmann asks his question, it really seems that he is suppressing anger. Surely not; is the objective Doctor actually annoyed? It is not clear at first

Feldmann What is the object of this—liaison, may I enquire?
Stephanie Fucking, I think. (*Slight pause for thought*) Yes. I think that's its main object, really.
Feldmann I did not ask you what the outcome of the liaison was, but its object.
Stephanie (*pondering*) Its object—its—object . . . hmm. Erm. Well, I suppose its object is having something to do the day after doing it the day before, if you follow me. I mean, it's something that's coming up. You know; tomorrow is another day, and so on.

Feldmann looks at her, grim-faced

I don't know why you're looking so disapproving. You just said yourself the purpose of life was life itself, and that there were lots of things to choose from. So see how clever I am; I did it even before you gave me your big lecture about it.

Feldmann Some purposes are of a positive and some of a negative nature, are they not?

Stephanie Well he's a very nice man, as a matter of fact. He's been married thirteen years and has two lovely looking boys, and he knows what he wants to do with his life. Surely you approve, don't you?

Feldmann Are you seeking my approval?

Stephanie Good heavens, no! But the idea of making this course of treatment, I think you called it, successful, is to tell all, isn't it, so that's what I'm doing.

Stephanie is looking forward to his answer in her miserable, destructive triumph. Pause

Feldmann And you feel this is a step forward, do you?

Stephanie Oh I'd say so, wouldn't you: getting out and about buying copper piping, learning about different metals, winning new friends and influencing people, wouldn't you say?

Slight pause

Feldmann (*still quiet*) This is a totally destructive activity, Miss Abrahams, as I'm sure you are only too well aware by your pathetically false tone of imposed normality.

Stephanie (*suddenly triumphant*) Ah ha! Do I detect morality rearing its ugly head? I thought the good Doctor remained entirely objective in all this. What is it? Don't we like the little girl indulging in extra-marital sex? Or—no, no. Of course! It's because it's with a totter, isn't it? It's the dirty totter we can't stand the thought of. Would it be all right with a judge or a company director, would it? Or a psychiatrist, perhaps? That would give it the stamp of respectability, of course, wouldn't it . . .?

Feldmann interrupts her in a hiss of seemingly genuine, quiet anger

Feldmann Don't play silly buggers with me, Miss Abrahams! I don't have the time for it, and I don't have the inclination! You think I just sit here dispensing pills and wisdom to keep my family in new dresses, well you're making a big mistake. We are engaged in a struggle here, Miss Madame; a struggle, yes. And you may pretend to yourself that you think that is very amusing and interesting and boring and sophisticated and other nonsense and rubbish, but that is not the case, and I would have kicked you and your money out long ago if it *were* the case. You think I am amused to hear you make flippant remarks about suicide and how many of my patients have killed themselves and other disgusting nonsense? You think because I sit here calmly and listen to all of it that I am just some kind of lay priest in the confessional box, here for your amusement or to unload the burden of your misfortune on to? Well you are totally and completely and stupidly *wrong*. For

your cynical information, some of my patients *have* committed suicide.
I have sat here and heard how the world and their families and society
have destroyed them and made them unhappy beyond the ability of
even a doctor to grasp. And then, because medical science and my skill
were inadequate, I have received news of their deaths; by hanging,
shooting, cutting their wrists in the bath, jumping from bridges, plung-
ing rusty knives into their bellies. And sometimes their husbands or
their wives or their children have come to me, and I have tried to
explain, to comfort, to restore some hope. So this is not my prime area
of comedy, you may possibly now understand. And, Miss Abrahams,
may I also inform you that is is *I* who am bored by *your* displays of
depression and cynicism and pretended unconcernedness, because they
are just stupid *games*, Miss Abrahams, stupid and boring games, which
hundreds of patients have tried to get me to play with them, but which
are simply symptoms of their unhappy condition, and so I resolutely
refuse to play these games with them. Because, Miss Abrahams, Mrs
Liebermann, the game here is a real one, a deadly earnest one, a life
and death game, as a matter of fact. Let me give it to you straight,
Madame, you are close to killing yourself. Yes. Very close. You are
walking the fine line. And you think you know this, but the unconscious
forces against which we struggle are actually pushing you far harder and
closer than you are aware. And do you think I shall sit back and allow
this enemy to triumph? No! We must give battle to these dark forces,
and I do, and I am asking you, or rather I am *telling* you, Miss Abrahams,
to add your weight to mine in this fight, and not to come in here with
childish displays of your sordid giving in to this enemy, dragging yourself and your self-esteem into the dirt in front of me, because all I see is
the slippery slope to despair, *and you will get off it, you hear me!* You
will get off it and you will fight beside me and that's *it*, you hear!?
(*Slight pause*) And you will resume with the medication I have prescribed immediately you leave here; is that clear!! Now cut it out, Miss
Abrahams. Get off your arse, if I may use your terminology; get off
your arse and fight!

*Feldmann stops and looks straight at Stephanie, who has been open-mouthed
with astonishment at this totally amazing turn of events in respect of Feldmann's manner. He stops, looks at her for a moment, then back down at the
desk. Silence. Stephanie feels as though she has been taken mentally to the
cleaners*

Stephanie (*eventually; straight and quiet*) I didn't know psychiatrists were
allowed to care personally what happened to their patients. I mean, I
thought getting involved was—was against the training, sort of thing.

Feldmann What makes you think I am involved and care personally.

Stephanie But—but—you mean you could be—that was, could have been
just a—a technique—a—a method?

Feldmann just looks straight at her. Pause

What's your first name, Dr Feldmann?

Feldmann I do not choose to talk on first-name terms with my patients.
Stephanie Oh I won't call you it. I just want to know what it is.
Feldmann Well. I suppose it's in the *Year Book*. My name is Alfred.
Stephanie (*after a pause*) You called me Stephanie just now . . .
Feldmann I had my reasons.

Pause

Stephanie I'm—I'm sorry I've been playing silly buggers. (*Pause*) Really.

Pause. Feldmann does not thank her, even with a gesture

I'll try to come over to your side in the—in the fight.

Feldmann speaks more quietly, but is still hard

Feldmann That means work, Miss Abrahams. You have to work at it.
There is nothing magic in this room, in these walls, in me, to make a
change, to find an answer. No musical magic, Madame. Just hard work,
inner work, and painful; more painful than what you are experiencing
now. But you are used to work as well as magic, are you not. Now you
must practise not on your violin eight hours, but on yourself, on your
inner themes and chords and progressions. Will you do it, and forget
all this terrible mental punk-rock you have been pouring out?
Stephanie (*quietly*) Yes. I will. Promise.

Feldmann looks at his watch

Feldmann We will resume next week.

*He rises. Both make for the door. Stephanie is trying to make her hair look
a bit better by patting and adjusting it. At the door she turns to him*

Stephanie Thank you . . .

Feldmann indicates she should go through ahead of him

Feldmann Please . . .

The Lights fade to a Black-out

SESSION 6

*Feldmann sits, reading a book, obviously waiting. The Bach plays on his
tape-deck. He looks at his watch, puts his book down, and, picking up a
watering-can goes round the room, watering his plants. He sits down at his
desk, looks at his watch again, and checks over some notes*

*The doorbell goes. Feldmann rises, checks the room, turns off the music, and
exits to the front door. He re-enters with Stephanie, as in the first session.
She is wearing a nice trouser suit, and looks smart. But under this, she is
very tense, though smiling. She seems, in much of the scene, to be somehow
alienated, strange*

When Stephanie is in her place, there is a long pause

Stephanie Sorry I'm late. (*Pause*) How are you? You're thinking "Aha. For the first time it is she who greets me; and her tone, her look, something has changed. Am I right? Yes." (*Pause*) Well, I was going through in my mind, you know, some of the things you were talking about last time—about, you know, life, activity, things to do, and the only thing which came to mind was private detective. I mean, there certainly was a time when I wanted to be one. From when I was ten to about twelve or thirteen, I think. (*Pause*) Just as a part of sort of looking behind things. But now I've just this vision of myself bursting open the door of a couple's room I was spying on, for a divorce case, and driving in and catching them in bed together, naked, and then the button of my chair motor sticks and I bang into the bed and get thrown out of the chair, and flop across the bed, and of course, I can't move, so I'm saying . . . (*Pause, while she thinks of what it is*) "This is a fair cop" or something, and the pair of them, completely naked, have to help me back into my chair. Well, it's ridiculous. But that's what you'd have me do, isn't it? Or something like it? You're just like my father. You're both employment agencies. He offered me jobs, as if playing the violin was some form of unemployment. And now you're the same, because you don't understand any better than he did. If you had, you wouldn't have bothered with me. (*Pause. She rises*) Dr Feldmann. Before I say—before I tell you . . . I mean. Well. I want to say I'm sorry for—for—what I'm going to say. Because you've been very kind. Or rather I mean you've been very human. And I'm sorry it can't be as you want, but I've made up my mind—I won't be coming back to see you again. I've decided to end the treatment. (*She sits in the armchair*) Playing the violin isn't a job, d'you see? It's not a job. It's other than that. When my mother died something special happened, do you see, something different. I used to come home from school and the first thing I did, before I took my coat off, or put the fire on, or made myself a cup of tea, the first thing I did was turn on the Third Programme. And I used to sit in the living-room alone, with the lights off, just the light from the radio shining, and I'd listen to whatever was on; symphonies, concertos, chamber-works, whatever. I did it to soothe me—to soothe away the pain. (*Pause*) Everything went when she died, everything, all the normal things, everything I was used to, all the bits and pieces of ordinary life went down the black hole along with Mummy. Daddy collapsed, stayed in bed, wouldn't go to work, wouldn't talk to me; one of the shops folded and my favourite shop-girl lost her job along with the others; we had to take in a lodger into Mummy's study; I was taken from my school and sent to one where we didn't have to pay; everything. Everything collapsed. Everything nice and safe; you've seen those people dug out from the rubble of an earthquake wandering around in a daze haven't you? (*Pause*) Look, Dr Feldmann, I played the violin, because when Mummy died, the real world; your world, the world of jobs, Daddy's world, it disappeared; shattered. So I had to build another world, what you'd call a fantasy world. My new world was filled with the pain and the sorrow and the despair of the loss and the awful unfamiliar changes. So I hung on to the only world I had: music. My violin. And I sang the song of the pain and the sorrow and loss and the awful changes, to soothe myself. And I sang for dear life—literally for life, 'cos it was all I had. And suddenly the song turned to one of joy, because of the beauty of the music; and I was ecstatic that I had turned such sorrow to happiness, because the change was such a relief, such a wonderful pleasure. And now I can't play any more. And because the shock and the pain were so awful again at this new loss, I tried to pretend I could cross back over to the old world and stupid little plans, like being David's secretary. But I'm not there, Dr Feldmann. The violin isn't my work; it isn't a way of life. It's where I live. It's when I play that I actually live in the real world; mine, of course. So what can you do? What can you possibly do, when I can't cross over? It's not your fault. It's not that you haven't got the skill. It's just that I'm over here—and I can't sing . . . (*She rises, walks slowly back to the wheelchair, sits*)

A very long pause

Feldmann Is the same time next week still convenient?

Stephanie turns sharply to look at Feldmann. They continue to look at each other, as the Lights fade to a Black-out, and—

the CURTAIN *falls*

FURNITURE AND PROPERTY LIST

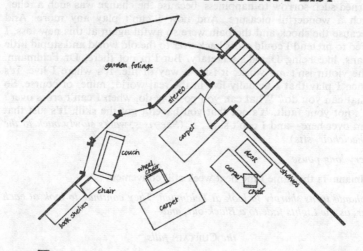

garden foliage

stereo

carpet

couch

wheel chair

chair

desk

carpet

shelves

carpet

chair

book shelves

carpet

ACT I

On stage: Desk. *On it:* writing materials, open pad, pen, file, prescription pad, family photos, telephone, Anglepoise lamp, sellotape holder, desk diary, tin of Meggezone tablets. *In drawer:* files. *Beside it:* waste-paper-basket

Wooden swivel desk chair

Armchair

Couch with pillow and coverlet

Shelves behind desk. *On them:* books, files, telephone directories, pot plants

Shelves near door. *On them:* music centre (practical), tapes (including Beethoven violin concerto), records, music books

Shelves by armchair. *On them:* books, bound journals

Filing cabinets

On window ledge: pot plants, watering can

On walls: various pictures

Carpets

Off stage: Electric wheelchair (Stephanie)

Personal: Feldmann: spectacles, wristwatch

ACT II

Chcek: File on desk

Tin of Meggezones

Water in watering can

Beethoven tape in prominent position on tape shelf

LIGHTING PLOT

Property fittings required: Anglepoise lamp, wall brackets (dressing only)
Interior. A consulting room. The same scene throughout

ACT I, SESSION 1

To open: General effect of mid-afternoon light

Cue 1   As Stephanie and Feldmann exit   (Page 8)
              Fade to Black-out

ACT I, SESSION 2

To open: As previous lighting

Cue 2   Stephanie exits: Feldmann stands for a moment   (Page 18)
              Fade to Black-out

ACT I, SESSION 3

To open: As previous lighting

Cue 3   Stephanie: "... change this condition with   (Page 25)
              determination ..."
              Fade to Black-out

ACT II, SESSION 4

To open: As previous lighting

Cue 4   Feldmann puts file on desk and goes to door   (Page 31)
              Fade to Black-out

ACT II, SESSION 5

Cue 5   Feldmann: "Please ..." (*They exit*)   (Page 37)
              Fade to Black-out

ACT II, SESSION 6

Cue 6   As Feldmann and Stephanie look at each other   (Page 39)
              Fade to Black-out

EFFECTS PLOT

ACT I

SESSION 1

Cue 1	Before CURTAIN rises *Music—Bach solo violin sonata on f.o.h. speakers*	(Page 1)
Cue 2	As CURTAIN rises *Transfer music to onstage speaker by cassette deck*	(Page 1)
Cue 3	After CURTAIN rises *Clock strikes three*	(Page 1)
Cue 4	**Feldmann** moves armchair into corner *Front doorbell rings*	(Page 1)
Cue 5	**Feldmann** stops tape *Cut music*	(Page ·1)

SESSION 2

No cues

SESSION 3

No cues

ACT II

SESSION 4

Cue 6	**Stephanie**: "Oh no—rotten bastard!" *Slight pause—clock strikes four*	(Page 30)
Cue 7	**Stephanie** wheels chair towards door *Front doorbell rings*	(Page 31)

SESSION 5

Cue 8	**Feldmann** puts tape on deck *Short burst of music, then switch off*	(Page 32)

SESSION 6

Cue 9	As Session opens *Bach sonata as opening of play*	(Page 37)
Cue 10	**Feldmann** sits at desk after watering plants *Pause—front doorbell rings*	(Page 37)
Cue 11	**Feldmann** stops tape *Cut music*	(Page 37)

MADE AND PRINTED IN GREAT BRITAIN BY
LATIMER TREND & COMPANY LTD PLYMOUTH
MADE IN ENGLAND